Drums around the World

Barbara Schubert

Dominie Press, Inc.

Publisher: Christine Yuen
Series Editors: Adria F. Klein & Alan Trussell-Cullen
Editors: Bob Rowland & Paige Sanderson
Photographer: Lois Stanfield
Illustrator: David Preston Smith
Designers: Gary Hamada & Lois Stanfield

Photo Credits: PhotoDisc (pages 6 and 10).

Copyright ©2001 Dominie Press, Inc. All rights reserved. No part of this publication may be reproduced or transmitted in any form or by any means without permission in writing from the publisher. Reproduction of any part of this book, through photocopy, recording, or any electronic or mechanical retrieval system, without the written permission of the publisher, is an infringement of the copyright law.

Published by:

Dominie Press, Inc.

1949 Kellogg Avenue
Carlsbad, California 92008 USA

www.dominie.com

ISBN 0-7685-0586-0

Printed in Singapore by PH Productions Pte Ltd

1 2 3 4 5 6 PH 03 02 01

ITP

Table of Contents

Reading about Drums	4
A Drum from Japan	6
A Drum for Battle	8
A Talking Drum	10
Making Our Own Drum	12
Picture Glossary	20
Index	20

David and Josie love drums. They are reading a book about drums.

"I want to have a drum of my own," said Josie.

"I do, too," said David.

Taiko Drum from Japan

"I want to have a drum like this," said David.

"You play it very hard and very fast," said their teacher.

Snare Drum

"I want to have a drum like this," said Josie.

"They had to play it loudly so it could be heard above the sounds of the battle," said their teacher.

**Talking Drum
from Africa**

"I want to have a drum like this," said David.

"You can send messages with it," said their teacher.

"Why don't you make your own drum?" asked their teacher.

"I will help you."

1.

3.

2.

14

How to Make a Drum

You will need:
- an oatmeal box
- a balloon
- a rubber band
- scissors

How to make it:
1. Cut the end off the balloon.
2. Stretch the balloon over the box.
3. Put a rubber band around the balloon.

Josie tapped the drum with her fingers. David tapped the drum with a pencil.

They listened to the sound.

"Which sound do you like best?" asked their teacher.

"We like both sounds that our drum makes!" said David and Josie.

Picture Glossary

Snare Drum:

Talking Drum:

Taiko Drum:

Index

balloon, 15

messages, 11

oatmeal box, 15

rubber band, 15

scissors, 15
Snare Drum, 8
sound(s), 17, 19

Taiko Drum, 6
Talking Drum, 10